ITIL® 2011 Foundation

A guide to passing the Exam on Your 1st Attempt!

DEDICATION

To my wife Rachel, who is my best friend. For all of her love and support and allowing me to move into my dream job of teaching. She is truly the most amazing women and I wouldn't be where I am or who I am without her by my side.

To my children, Daniel, I am proud of the husband you have become to Maria, and to Vanessa, you have grown up so much and are an amazing wife to Rene and mother to my little best mate, my grandson Conner

Thank You

"If you can't explain it simply, you don't understand it well enough!!"
Albert Einstein

Copyright & Legal Information

ACKNOWLEDGEMENTS

I wholeheartedly blame ILX Group, whom I am an associate consultant and Gen B, who pushed me into teaching ITIL. Which then led to me complaining about how boring the material was to teach, so to fix this, I have written this book to support the official material and to support the students who I teach and anyone wishing to learn ITIL.

I hope you find this book useful and the contents help you starting your ITIL Journey.

INTRODUCTION

The objectives are to enable you to:

- **_Understand_** how this book is designed to help you pass your certification exam quickly
- **_Understand_** how the exam is designed and how to take the certification exam
- **_Understand_** some tips and tricks for conquering the ITIL® 2011 Foundation exam

Welcome to the book, you're here for the simple reason you have made the decision to either learn about the Information Technology Infrastructure Library (ITIL®) 2011 or to undertake the actual exam. The aim of this book is to provide you with a crash course that gives you enough information in order to pass the ITIL® 2011 Foundation exam

This book is designed to be short, sharp and cover the essentials without any filler or fluff. This has often been some of the feedback when teaching ITIL® 2011 Foundation, "there are too many slides, its death by PowerPoint, it's too wordy!"

The overall requirement I wrote on the wallboard in my office at home when starting to write this book – to be able to learn the material in a quick and simple way that will allow you to pass the exam on the 1st attempt

This book also assumes that you have little or no previous experience with the ITIL® 2011 framework and aims to teach you the bare minimum you need to know in order to take and pass the ITIL® 2011 Foundation certification exam on your first attempt

This book will **NOT** teach you everything you need to know to be efficient or effective in implementing the ITIL® 2011 Framework within your organisation. It is designed to help you to pass the certification exam, not to make you an expert in ITIL®, that will take time, experience and more reading

Due to the design and style of this book, you will move at a very quick pace through the material, and the information is presented in such a way that it should be easy to read and understand

When you finish reading this entire book and then take the practice exam located at the end of the text (scoring at least an 85% or higher), you will be ready to take and pass the ITIL® 2011 Foundations exam on your first attempt!

Exam Basics

The ITIL® 2011 Foundation exam is an entry-level certification for the Information Technology Service Management (ITSM) discipline. The foundation certification covers a general awareness of the elements, concepts, and terminology used in the ITIL® Service Lifecycle and IT Service Management.

The target audience for the ITIL® 2011 Foundations certification is:

- People requiring an understanding of the ITIL® framework
- People needing an understanding of how ITIL® can enhance IT service management within an organisation
- IT professionals in organisations that adopted ITIL® and need to understand ongoing service improvement

The exam consists of 40 multiple-choice questions which must be completed within 60 minutes.

A minimum score of 26 out of 40 questions is required to pass the certification exam, equating to a score of 65% or higher.

The exam is a closed book exam, with no notes or study materials being allowed to be brought into the examination centre.

To sit for the exam, you must sign up through either an Accredited Training Organisation (ATO) or directly through People Cert. The exam can be taken in the classic classroom environment or online using a web invigilator. My personal recommendation is the classroom, I simply find the web process more stressful (and also a little weird)

Exam Tips & Tricks

Before we dig into the content of the ITIL® 2011 Foundation exam, it is important for you to read through some exam tips and tricks. These will help you understand exactly how to study for the exam as you read through the book and focus your efforts to get the most out of this material.

The most important thing to remember when taking the ITIL® 2011 Foundation exam is that there are no trick questions. Every question is precisely worded to match the material you have studied. You should read the question at least twice to ensure you understand exactly what the question is asking you, and that you are answering the question being asked, not what you think is being asked, which is what I have seen on numerous times when teaching.

If you see the words *ALWAYS* or *NEVER* in an answer, think twice about selecting it. In IT Service Management, rarely is there a case where something *ALWAYS* or *NEVER* applies to the situation!

As you read the questions and answers, always be on the lookout for distractors or red herrings. Generally, there is at least one of these listed in the possible answers to try and distract you.

If you see a question with bold, italics, or in all uppercase, you should pay close attention to those words because the examiners have decided they are keywords and very important to selecting the correct answer. I personally always highlight these to ensure I focus upon that

It is also important to remember what things in the ITIL® 2011 Framework are processes, and which are functions. We will cover both throughout this book. If a question asks about a process, make sure you don't select an answer that contains a function or a service.

Another important thing to remember is that you must answer the questions based on your ITIL® knowledge and studies from this textbook, not your personal workplace experience. Your workplace may not be implementing ITIL® correctly in their IT Service Management operations, so you must always select the book answer when answering a question on the exam. Remember the exam is asking relating to the book, not the real world or your organisations implementation

Remember that on exam day, you should select the BEST answer. Each question may have several right answers, but one is always the "most right answer". When in doubt, choose the answer that is correct in the most number of situations!

On test day, you don't have to memorize the definitions from the ITIL® 2011 Framework word for word, but you must be able to recognize them from the choices given. This is an essential difference in IT Certification testing where the answers are multiple-choice and the tests you may have taken in high school or college where you had to fill in a blank or write a short answer. In the IT Certification world, you must be able to recognize, not regurgitate, the information.

As you study the material in this book, keep these objectives in mind:
- Know generic process model and process characteristics
- Be able to differentiate between service, process, and function

Finally, remember that if you get asked about the service owner or process owner, verify your answer matches the question asked. If the question asks about a process, DO NOT select an answer with the word service in it!

ITSM AND THE ITIL® FRAMEWORK

The objectives of this chapter are to enable you to:

- **Understand** IT Service Management and the fundamentals of the ITIL® 2011 Framework
- **Name** the 5 phases of the Service Lifecycle
- **Understand** the characteristics of processes in ITIL® 2011
- **Understand** the characteristics of functions in ITIL® 2011
- **Understand** the standard roles in ITIL® 2011
- **Understand** organisational structures and their relation to ITIL® 2011
- **Understand** the various types of service desks in ITIL® 2011
- **Understand** the Technical Management function
- **Understand** the Application Management function
- **Understand** the IT Operations Management function
- **Understand** the RACI Model

The definition of IT Service Management (ITSM) is the complete set of activities required to provide value to a customer through services, including policies and strategies to Plan, Design, Deliver, Operate, and Control IT services

This leads us to question, what is a service? The definition of a service according to ITIL®

"A Service is a means of delivering value to customers by facilitating the outcomes customers want to achieve without the ownership of specific costs and risk"

For example, if your organisation wants a website to allow customers to buy its services 24 hours a day, 7 days a week, but does not have the skills or facilities needed to host it or want the associated expenses. It decides instead to pay a service provider" to run the website on its behalf. Your organisation pays a fee to the service provider. In essence your organisation has received the desired outcome without the ownership of the specific costs or risks

There are many different IT Service Management (ITSM) models and frameworks, but we are only going to focus on the Information Technology Infrastructure Library (ITIL®). ITIL® was developed as a framework for organisations to use in order to perform effective ITSM.

Not surprisingly, on the ITIL® 2011 Foundations certification exam, the only ITSM framework that is tested is the ITIL® 2011 framework.

The ITIL® framework is made up of the best practices from throughout the IT industry. The easiest and simplest definition of best practices is "that they are proven activities or processes that have been successfully used by many different organisations in a specific industry"

These best practices can come from multiple sources, including standards, industry practices or processes, academic research, training and education, and internal employee experiences.

THE SERVICE LIFECYCLE

The ITIL® 2011 Framework is built around the Service Lifecycle. This lifecycle consists of 5 phases:

1. Service Strategy,
2. Service Design,
3. Service Transition,
4. Service Operation,
5. Continual Service Improvement.

There are many ways to visualize these five phases and how they work together. The official ITIL® 2011 Framework depicts it as follows:

Figure 1 - IT Service Lifecycle

While this lifecycle diagram is useful, it doesn't really depict the reality of the ITIL® 2011 Service Lifecycle as it is used in the real world, it shows the diagram in amore pictorial fashion. Instead, I prefer to diagram the lifecycle with an opportunity for continuously feedback within each stage, as shown in the modified lifecycle diagram below

:

The diagram above represents a more real world view of the ITIL Lifecycle

Figure 2 - Modified Service Lifecycle

As shown in the diagram, each service begins in Service Strategy, then moves through the lifecycle.

At each and every point, there is an opportunity for continuous feedback supporting the Continual Service Improvement phase. Where those changes can be implemented in earlier stages (for the next version of a given service). This encapsulates the essence of Continual Service Improvement, and more closely reflects the reality you will experience in real-world IT Service Management.

Each phase of this service lifecycle will be covered in-depth in subsequent chapters of this book. As we cover each phase, we will also cover its associated processes and functions to ensure you are ready for those questions on exam day.

Processes
The definition of a **process** is

"A set of coordinated activities combining resources and capability to produce an outcome that creates value for the customer"

In the ITIL® 2011 Framework, there are 26 distinct processes covered throughout the 5 phases of the service lifecycle. However, only 22 of these processes are covered in-depth by the Foundations exam.

Each process has the same four characteristics.
1. They must respond to a specific event, called a trigger.
2. They must be measurable by using metrics like performance, cost, productivity, quality, and duration.
3. They must produce a specific result.
4. They must deliver a result to a defined customer to meet expectations.

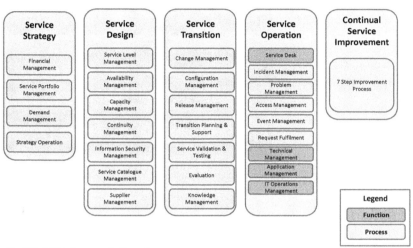

Figure 3 - ITIL 2011 Process & Functions

The diagram above shows a complete list of all of the processes and functions covered within the ITIL® 2011 Foundation exam. Each of these processes and functions will be covered later in this book as we cover the 5 phases of the service lifecycle in their own chapters.

Each process can be depicted using a three-layered model containing its process control, the process itself, and the process enablers.

- The process controls include process policies, ownership, documentation, review programs, etc.

- The process itself contains the steps of the process, procedures, work instructions, roles, triggers, metrics, inputs, and outputs.
- The process enablers include resources and capabilities that are required to support the process.

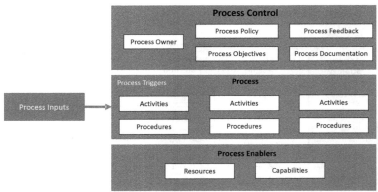

Figure 4 - 3 Layer Process Model

Functions

The definition of a **Function** is

"Functions are a self-contained unit of an organisation specialized that perform specific tasks and are responsible for an outcome"

These functions actually perform the activities of processes and they consist of a group of people and the tools they use to create a given outcome through a process.

What makes a process different than a function?

In essence, processes help organisations achieve certain objectives, even across multiple functional groups, whereas functions, add stability and structure to the organisation by being mapped to the organisational chart, having an assigned budget, and defined reporting structures associated

In most organisations, processes often rely on multiple functions to accomplish their outcomes. Processes and functions are both very intertwined, and processes would not be effective without supporting functions. Additionally, both processes and functions have roles associated with them, these will be covered in later chapters.

Roles

The definition of a **Role**

"Roles are a collection of specific responsibilities, duties, or positions within a process or function"

Each role can be held or assigned to an individual, individuals or a team of individuals. Effectively meaning a single person or team can have more than one role assigned.

In the ITIL® 2011 Framework, there are four standard roles that are utilized: service owner, process owner, service manager, and the process manager.

Service Owner - The Service Owner is accountable for:

The overall design, performance, integration, improvement, and management of a single service.

They are responsible for:
- The initiation, transition, and maintaining of the service;
- Ensuring service delivery is met;
- Identifying service improvements;
- Being the liaison to the Process Owners;
- Reporting and monitoring;
- Overall accountability for delivering the service.

Process Owner - The process owner is accountable for the overall design, performance, integration, improvement, and management of a single process. They are responsible for:

- Initiation, transition, and maintaining of the process;
- Defining the process strategy and policy;
- Assisting in the process design;
- Ensuring the process is documented;
- Auditing the process for efficiency;
- Communicating the process to others;
- Provisioning resources and training;
- Inputting suggestions into the service improvement program.

Service Manager - The service manager is accountable for:
The development, performance, and improvement of all services.

Process manager - is accountable for the development, performance, and improvement of all processes.

There are two additional roles that are not considered part of the standard roles, these are the roles of product manager and the process practitioner.

Product Manager - The product manager is accountable for the development, performance, and improvement of a group of related services.

Process Manager - The process practitioner is responsible for actually conducting the actions and functions associated with operating the service. For example, the person answering the phones in the service desk may be considered a process practitioner for the Service Request Fulfilment process.

The following roles are not considered standard roles, the **Product Manager** who is accountable for the development, performance and improvement of a group of (related) services.

The **Process Practitioner** is responsible for actually conducting the actions and functions associated with operating the service.

Organisational Structure

Whenever I teach ITIL® 2011, the biggest and most often asked questions relates to the organisation of the teams to support ITIL® 2011. In essence this is ITIL® 2011 does not provide any model for the structure of the teams or the workforce.

ITIL® 2011 provides guidance on the structure, but this is not necessarily prescriptive, in truth each volume of the ITIL® 2011 Framework has chapter 6 "guidance on the organisational structure", these chapters contain roles and responsibilities listed. However, these are more of a checklist when considering the roles and not a requirement as to what roles are needed for ITIL® 2011

This then leads to the next question (and when I teach is often with a puzzled look!) if ITIL® 2011 doesn't provide a structure, what should we doing. There are a few very crucial things to consider when thinking about the organisational structure

Firstly, the roles (as detailed earlier) can be filled by multiple people, and one person can fulfil many different roles. When assigning roles, it is important to ensure that you review the assignments and ensure there are no gaps in the assigned responsibilities. Always ensure that all roles required are filled by someone inside your organisation.

ITIL® focuses on the relationships between functions and processes, and between the fours standard roles. Much of the focus in ITIL® is placed on the four major functions that support the various processes: Service Desk, Technical Management, Application Management, and IT Operations Management.

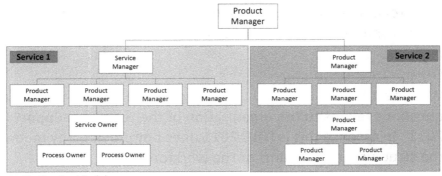

Figure 5 - Service Model

Service Desk

The **Service Desk** provides a single, central point of contact for all users of IT services. The is the first point of contact for all issues with all services, including inbound incidents, service requests, change requests, and much more. Usually, the service desk also owns the Incident Management process, since they are the first call by a customer when something goes wrong with a given service.

Many organisations have a help desk, while others have a service desk, but what is the difference?

Firstly, service desks are simply call centres or help desks. These help desks really focus on answering customer calls and fixing broken services for the customers. Over time, these help desks become better organized and evolve into a full-blown service desks, offering more than just a "break-fix" mentality to problem solving.

These service desks became the singular point of focus for customers, handling break-fix issues, upgrades, training, and much more.

There are four major types of service desk models: Local Service Desk, Centralised Service Desk, Virtual Service Desk, and Follow-the-Sun.

Local Service Desk - The local service desk is physically located close to the customers they support. Usually, they reside in the same building or offices as their customers, such as an embedded IT support person inside the accounting department, or even a singular service desk to support the entire building.

Figure 6 - Local Service- Desk

Centralised Service Desk - The centralised service desk model makes better use of resources, improves consistency, and centralizes management. Under this model, a single service desk would remotely answer all telephone support calls, regardless of the location of the customer.

Figure 7 - Centralised Service Desk

Virtualised Service Desk - The virtualised service desk doesn't require a centralised location, but can still make better use of resources, improves consistency, and centralises management. Under this model, the location of the service desk personnel is irrelevant and could even include remote home-based teleworkers. Customers simply call a centralised telephone support number and their call is routed to the next available agent, regardless of the customer's or agent's location.

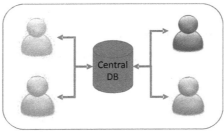

Figure 8 - Virtualised Service-Desk

Follow the Sun - The follow-the-sun service desk model combines local, centralized, and virtual service desks, allowing for 24x7 coverage across all time zones. As shown below, during the normal business hours the calls are routed to a call centre in that time zone (for example, a New York support desk during office hours in the United States). If a United States customer calls for service after normal business hours, their call is routed to a different call centre (for example, to England or Japan based on the normal working hours of those service desk locations).

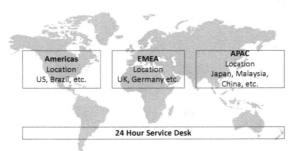

Figure 9 - Follow-the-Sun

Technical Management

The **Technical Management** function is responsible for the procurement, development, and management of the technical skill sets and resources required to support the infrastructure and the ITSM efforts. This function provides technical resources to all phases of the ITIL® 2011 Lifecycle.

The Technical Management function ensures that the Service Provider has the right skill sets available to deliver the services it offers to its customers. Generally, Technical Management is divided into specialty areas, such as networking, security, databases, storage, servers, and other specialized fields required to support the overall service provider objectives.

Application Management

The **Application Management** function provides end-to- end management of applications in the environment and involves cultivating the skill sets and resources to support all phases of the lifecycle. Application Management also helps to identify software requirements and their sourcing (internal/external).

Application Management is focused on the ongoing oversight, operational management, and improvement of applications for both utility and warranty.

Application Development, on the other hand, is focused on design and construction of an application solution to gain initial utility.

Application Management is a function that supports and does not replace other core processes, such as Incident Management, Problem Management, Change Management, Availability Management, and many others.

IT Operations Management

The **IT Operations Management** function provides a stable platform on which services can be delivered to meet the agreed-upon business needs. It performs the day-to-day running of the IT infrastructure and the facilities that house it and is split into two sub-functions: Operations Control and Facilities Management.

Operations Control monitors the infrastructure for optimal performance minute-by-minute and conducts the normal maintenance cycles required. To do this, operations controls performs Console Management, backup and restoral operations, media management, batch job execution, and more.

These operations are usually controlled from the Network Operations Centre (NOC) or the Operations Bridge. An example of these work centres is shown in the photograph below:

Unlike Operations Control, **Facilities Management** is only concerned with physical environment of the IT infrastructure, including the power, cooling, fire suppression, and physical access to the data centres and server rooms. To be effective, though, the facilities management team must have a close working relationship with the Operations Control watch team. In many organisations, both the Operations Control and Facilities Management personnel are collocated in the same workspaces.

The RACI Model

The **RACI Model** is a generic tool for reviewing and assigning four key roles to any activity: Responsible, Accountable, Consulted, and Informed.

Each activity can have many roles who are assigned responsible, consulted, and informed, however only one role can be listed as accountable. As the old saying goes,

If everyone is accountable, then nobody is accountable!

The RACI Model provides a visual indication of the linkages between roles, their responsibility, and the accountability for a given task in a process.

Responsible (R) refers to the person who executes or performs the activity.
Accountable (A) refers to the person who owns the activity and must answer for its outcomes.

Only a single person can be held accountable for a given activity. **Consulted** (C) refers to the person who reviews and provides advice and authorization for the activity.
Informed (I) refers to the person who receives updates on activity's progress.

A simplified version of a **R**esponsible, **A**ccountable, **C**onsulted, and **I**nformed (RACI) Matrix is provided as an example:

Roles & Responsibilities Matrix	1. Portfolio Production Executive	2. Project Sponsor	2.1 Project Executive	2.2 Project Sponsor	2.3 ADM	2.4 ABM	2.4 CIO	2.4.1 Head of IT	2.4.2 Business Partner	2.5 Project assurance	3.1 IT Project Manager	3.1 IT P
P1 - Portfolio Deveoplment												
New Project Assesment (NPA)	R	I	C	I	C	A						A
High Level Requirements	I	I	C	I	C	A						A
Project Plan (Stage 1-4)	I	I	C	I	C	A						A
Business Case (Draft)	I	I	C	I	C	A						A
Benefits Model (Draft)	I	I	C	I	C	A						A
Weekly Report	I	I	C	I	C	A						A
Fortnightly Report	I	I	C	I	C	A						A
Financial Estimates (Draft)	I	I	C	I	C	A						A
Project Stage Plan	I	I	C	I	C	A						A
Project Org Chart	I	I	C	I	C	A						A
P2 - Business Case Development												
Final Business Case												

Figure 10 - RACI MATRIX

SERVICE STRATEGY PHASE

Overview
Service Strategy describes an IT organization's high-level approach to providing services. First, the IT organization must identify the market for its services. This, in turn, drives the identification of services offerings as well as the strategic assets that will constitute those services. Envisioned services will be added to the service portfolio. These identified services will continue to be pursued until they are finally chartered for design (and development), which moves those services into the Service Design stage.

Supporting this overall activity is the need to determine the IT organisation's overall approach to providing services. This may include internal providers, external providers, a shared approach, preferred providers, etc. In addition, several practices play a part in determining the overall service strategy, including financial management, demand management, and risk management.

Objectives

The objectives of this chapter are to enable you to:

- **Describe and understand** the Service Strategy phase
- **Describe** a business case analysis
- **Describe** value, utility, and warranty
- **Describe** service assets
- **Describe** the Service Portfolio Management process
- **Describe** the Strategy Management process
- **Describe** the Demand Management Process
- **Describe** the Financial Management Process

The **Service Strategy** phase establishes and manages the broadest policies and standards to govern how a service provider will operate. This will determine the selection of services a service provider will offer to its customers. All services should deliver value to customers, enable the service providers to capture value, be of acceptable cost to the service provider, and be of acceptable risk to the service provider.

Remember the definition of a service? (You better), because it will come up again and again!

"A service is a means of providing value to customers by facilitating the outcomes they want to achieve without the ownership of specific costs and risks".

Now, the Service Strategy phase aims to creates value to the service provider and its customer by offering services that are aligned with business objectives and are likely to offer value. Also, these services should allow for customers to be charged for their use or give the service provider another beneficial (non-monetary) outcome. At the end of the day, the service provider must be able to handle the costs and risks associated with offering the service, otherwise they could go out of business.

In the Service Strategy phase, there are four processes we must learn:

1. Service Portfolio Management
2. Strategy Management
3. Financial Management
4. Demand Management

Business Case Analysis

Business Case Analysis is the structured and documented justification for a new investment that argues the benefits and costs of a particular service. Each time you create a new or changing service, you should create a business case analysis to determine the expected Return on Investment (ROI) for the service

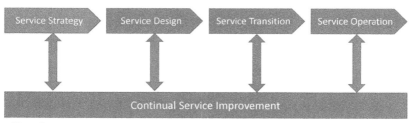

The diagram above represents a more real world view of the ITIL Lifecycle

Figure 11 - ITIL Service Lifecycle

There are five parts to a business case analysis:

1. Introduction,
2. Methods and Assumptions
3. Business impacts
4. Risks and contingencies
5. Recommendations.

Each business case analysis will make a case for a new or changed service based on either its return on investment (ROI) or value on investment (VOI).

The **return on investment** (ROI) is the expected financial growth created by a service, or more simply, the amount of money returned to the service provider after its costs of providing a given service.

The **value on investment** (VOI) is the expected non-financial return created by a service, such as in a service provider's increased recognition or reputation.

Value, Utility & Warranty

Value is created from the balance between utility and warranty. A service must have both utility and warranty in order to create value for a customer.

The **utility** of a service is its *fit for purpose*. This refers to the functionality of a service or its ability to enable a job to be done. Utility is important because it removes the constraints faced by a customer or increasing the customer's overall performance through a given service.

The **warranty** of a service is its *fit for use*. This refers to the mix of availability, capacity, continuity, and security of a given service. While utility sells services, without warranty a service will fail to operate and create issues for your customers.

To create maximum value, you attempt to find the perfect balance to create the most value. Utility and warranty are always equally as important, it is always dependent on the customer requirements and the service being provided.

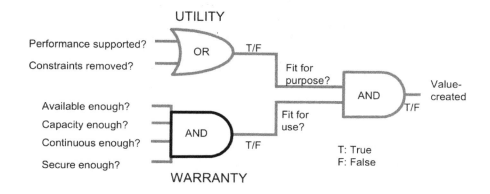

Figure 12 - Utility, Warranty, Value

There are three examples of value as a balance of utility and warranty below.

In the first example, we have poor value because we have a website that was created with all the latest technology and the best features (high utility), but the infrastructure was built poorly and results in limited bandwidth to support the site (poor warranty) and thereby creates poor overall value to the customer.

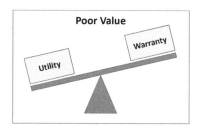

In the second example, we have another example of poor value to the customer. In this example, the database designer created a horribly inefficient design that doesn't meet all the customer's needs (low utility). The infrastructure, though, was built with a highly redundant and available backbone (creating high warranty). As shown in the graphic, the overall result is poor value to the customer.

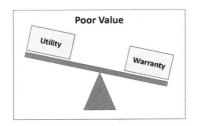

In the third example, we see a good balance of utility and warranty, resulting in a maximum value for the customer. This is the perfect balance we seek to achieve, with the optimal amount of utility (fit for purpose) and warrant (fit for use).

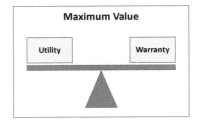

Every time a service is added or changed, it is important to consider the utility and warranty of that service. Remember, that while utility *sells* services, it is the warranty that really requires the resources to support the service, and therefore represents an increase in costs.

Service Assets

Service assets are resources and capabilities which the service provider must allocate to provide a given service.

Resources are tangible items that contribute to a service. These can be purchased with financial capital, such as raw materials, infrastructure, applications, information, and even people (labour).

Capabilities are specialized skills or abilities that are applied by organisation to add value. These are the intangibles of a company, such as its management, organisation, processes, and skills.

Service Portfolio Management Process

The **Service Portfolio Management Process** is concerned with managing the services that comprise the service portfolio. This is where services are organized, identified, described, evaluated, selected, and charted, as well as their place in the service portfolio.

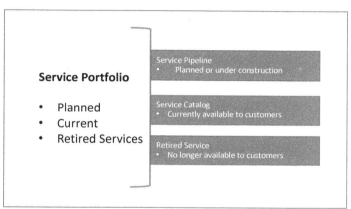

Figure 13 - Service Portfolio

The **Service Portfolio** is the complete set of services under management by a service provider. The service portfolio is comprised of three major sections: the service pipeline, service catalog, and retired services.

The service portfolio's purpose is to help the service provider understand how its resources are used to maximize value. All resources are allocated to services throughout their lifecycle from the IT director's resource pool. As services move into the Service Operation phase, they will usually use more resource than they did in earlier stages. In fact, many services use over 70% of their resources and budget just in the Service Operations phase!

Strategy Management Process

The **Strategy Management Process** ensures a service strategy is defined, maintained, and managed. This process focuses on the development of service concepts in preparation for selection of

services to be provided and is also known as the Strategy
Operation Process in some ITIL® books.

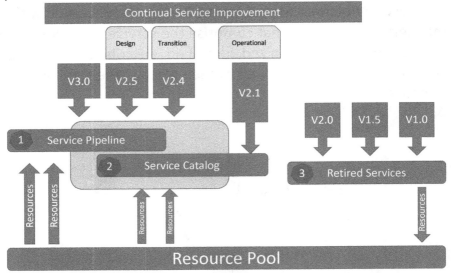

Figure 14 - Strategy Management Process

In the Strategy Management Process, there are several keys
activities that occur.

First, the organisation seeks to understand the current
marketplace. They do this by asking questions such as "who the
customer is", "what they value", and "how the customer defines
value".

Next, the offerings and services are developed by asking
questions such as "what services could be offered to provide
value to our customers" and "how we can offer a unique or
distinctive value in the marketplace".

During this process, strategic assets are also developed by
determining the appropriate resources and capabilities to apply to
the proposed service. To best determine this, questions are asked,
such as "what resources would be required to offer the proposed
service" and "what capabilities would be needed to provide the
service".

Finally, the service execution is prepared for by outlining the broad scope of the service's objectives. The specific questions considered during this activity is things like "how we can prepare to develop the service", "what the service objectives are", and "what critical success factors must be met to achieve our objectives". During Service Design, this broad scope is further defined and narrowed as the service is designed more fully.

Demand Management Process

The **Demand Management Process** is used to identify the demand for a particular service to prevent capacity limitations. Understanding the demands of your customers is important to the service provider, unmanaged demand is a cost and risk to the service provider.

For example, if you planned to support 1,000 visitors to a website per day using 1 Mb of data, but instead you had a surge in demand to 100,000 visitors per day and they used 1 Gb of data, you could face cost and budget overruns for excessive bandwidth utilization dependent upon your contracts

During the Demand Management Process, the patterns of business activity are identified and analysed. This utilization of the service is analysed to help determine the different types of users and their patterns, helping to identify and document user profiles for your customers and helping to better predict the future demands on the service.

Understanding the patterns of business activity is extremely important, because businesses always have busy and slow periods. Building your service around a peak period could cause additional costs to the company for the resources required to maintain these services

Financial Management Process

The **Financial Management Process** is used to understand and manage financial resources, costs, and opportunities for a service. Proper financial management helps to provide and organisation with a clear method of generating data to aid in management decisions.

One of the most important functions of the financial management process is to secure funding to design, develop, and deliver services to support business processes and to ensure service provider doesn't promise what they cannot deliver. Financial management is all about maintaining a balance of cost and quality, as well as a balance of supply and demand.

There are three major activities in the financial management: budgeting, accounting, and charging.

- **Accounting** is the tracking of money by cost centres and against the original budget.
- **Budgeting** is the forecasting and planning of how to spend money in relation to providing a service.
- **Charging** is how an organisation gets payment from the customers for services.

Remember, with charging, it doesn't have to refer to an external customer. Some organisations require departments to reimburse other departments on a *fee for service* model by using charging against the serviced departments budget to offset the costs incurred by the servicing department.

SERVICE DESIGN PHASE

Overview

Service Design is a stage in the service lifecycle in which a new or modified service is developed and made ready for the Service Transition stage.

The primary effort of this stage is the design (and development) of the service. This include defining service requirements, designing the service solution, evaluating alternate suppliers of the service, and integrating existing service assets or creating them from scratch into a service.

Service Level Management provides the interface to IT customers in the collection of requirements. Supporting processes such as Availability Management, Capacity Management, Information Security Management, and IT Service Continuity Management are consulted to make sure the envisioned service will meet service level targets and expectations. Supplier Management man- ages relationships with potential service providers.

As the service progresses through this stage, the Service Catalog is updated with new information about the service, including status changes in the service. The Service Catalog is that part of the Service Portfolio that can be viewed by IT customers. It is al- so an instrument of Service Level Management to enter into discussions with IT customers about new service requirements or about the initiation of a service level agreement.

Objective

The objectives of this chapter are to enable you to:
- Describe and understand the Service Design phase
- Describe a business value in terms of the Service Design
- Describe quality on Service Design
- Describe the 4 P's of Service Design
- Describe the Service Catalog Management Process
- Describe the Service Catalog types
- Describe the Service Level Management Process
- Describe the Availability Management Process
- Describe the Capacity Management Process
- Describe the Information Security Management Process

- Describe the Supplier Management Process

The Service Design phase conducts the detailed planning of the service and all supporting requirements to allow a successful transition into the operational environment. During the Service Design phase, the following questions are answered:
- How will the service be supported?
- How will the service be tested?
- How will the service be developed in the future?

By the completion of the Service Design phase, a service design plan (SDP) is created and passed to the Service Transition team. The SDP should be a comprehensive, detailed and well communicated plan that is reviewed and agreed by all service stakeholders. This plan is a blueprint that includes the components of the service, the resources that may be shared with existing services, a structured test plan that identifies any specialist skills or resources needed, a support plan and a future development plan

Within Service Design, the organization is primarily concerned with creating an effective service, although at this stage the efficiency of the service is not a primary concern. This efficiency will increase over time through the use of the Continuous Service Improvement Process.

The Service Design has 5 aspects the should be considered,
1. Consider the actual service itself
2. Consider what Service Management processes are needed to support the service
3. Determine the which Service Management systems and tools are needed to support the service
4. Define the technology architecture which will be used by the service
5. Create the measurement systems and metrics that will be utilized to understand the performance of the new service

Within Service Design, you must learn the 7 processes
1. Service Catalog Management
2. Service Level Management
3. Capacity Management
4. Continuity Management
5. Information Security Management
6. Supplier Management

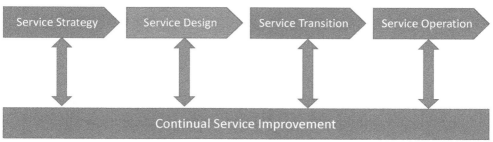

Figure 15 - Service Design

Business Value in Service Design

The primary goal of all Service Designs is to ensure that the services being created are aligned with the business objectives in order to ensure maximum value. Each service should provide the agreed Utility and Value to meet the objectives identified during the Service Strategy Phase

For a service to become effective and efficient, the organization must ensure that its Service Management processes are capable of supporting the service. If they do not support the proposed service offering, then the overall business value will suffer

It is important that all services are built to the align to agreed architectural and are designed to ensure that the performance of the service is adequately measured. The provision of continuous metrics and measurements ensures that a service can be assessed as to its overall success or failure and that the measurements are quantifiable. This aids in the management decision as to whether the service is meeting the agreed objectives and should continue to be supported or if it should be retired

Quality in Service Design

Quality must be considered early in the Service Design phase in order to create the best services. It is imperative to consider the entire service holistically to ensure its quality is created and understood by the whole team. Clearly defined specifications for what level of quality must be achieved are a necessity if you are going to develop a quality service. It is also important to ensure that the process exist to support the warranty of the service (ensuring it is fit for use)

During the Service Design Phase, it is important to focus upon quality, whilst it is the view of most people that these flaws can be rectified at a later stage in the process, it is often much more difficult and can be costlier to fix these design flaws during Service Transition or Service Operation.

Remember, once you are in the Service Operation Phase, your customer is experiencing or using the service. With this in mind you want to ensure the service is designed of sufficient quality, so it is crucial to design it right first time!

The 4P's of Service Design

When designing a service, there are four essential P's that must be considered

1. People
2. Processes
3. Products
4. Partners

People – People consist of the technical staff, users, customers, stakeholders, executives and many others. People need to be trained, managed, supervised, hired, fired and convinced. People are essential to the ITIL lifecycle and the success of the service

Processes – Processes for the very basis for ITIL in the ITIL® 2011 lifecycle, there are 26 distinct processes that are being utilized. During Service Design it is important to consider the processes that a new service will interact with or utilize

Products – Products are made up of other services, technology (hardware, software, Networks etc) and these tolls need to be capable of supporting the service. These products can be built in-house or purchased externally

Partners – Partners are people or organizations that help the Service Provider to provide these services, these can include suppliers, manufacturers, vendors, associates or any other business that are needed by the Service Provider

Service Catalog Management Process

The Service Catalog Management Process is the management and control of the Service Catalog. The Service Catalog is effectively a database or a document that contains all of the information relating to live services and those services that have been retired. This enables stakeholders to have a clear understanding of the services provided that support the business objectives

The Service Catalog contains information on the service, usage guidelines, access methods, pricing information (which can be part of a restricted access view), Points of contact, support information, service level information or agreements

The benefits relating to a well-structured and produced Service Catalog increase with the number of services supported or provided by an organisation, it helps to identify services that could be bundled allowing you to provide more effective solutions. It can provide additional information to support sales or business relationship services, it can also provide information for service or support staff about a service allowing them to better understand the service and their role in the support of it.

Another benefit is information in relation to services that are due to be rolled out or enter live operations in the future, which can better manage the expectations of the customer

Whilst the Service Catalog is used heavily in the Service Operations phase of the lifecycle, it is created during the Service Design phase and updated when new services are being planned as part of the Service Design Package creation. The Catalog structure is managed and its contents are modified during the Service Design and it is during this phase that the Catalog is checked to ensure it is complete, accurate and the data contained is current. As the service is design, any proposed changes to the catalog are reviewed prior to being authorised, the primary reason that the Service Catalog management occurs during Service Design is that it is during this phase that the majority of the information and documentations for the service is created, and this information should be placed into the Service Catalog to allow the new or changed service to be supported

In the ITIL® 2011 Foundation there are four types of Service Catalog
1. Simple Service
2. Business or Customer
3. Technical or Supporting
4. Alternate Views

- **Simple Service Catalog** – is a simplified matrix or list of the services that includes the most up to date, comprehensive and accurate information
- **Business or Customer Facing Service Catalog** – identifies the business processes that are being supported by the services and details can include the service hours, SLA information, key Points of Contact, escalation paths, third party support information

- **Technical or Supporting Service Catalog** – provides the lower level of detail supporting the infrastructure, application's, outsourced services etc
- **Alternate View Service Catalog** – is displayed in various formats as needed, examples are the 3-view model, which includes the Technical or Supporting view, the Business view and Financial services information

Service Level Management Process

The Service Level Management Process aims at securing and managing the agreement between the Service Provider and the Customer in relation to the utility (level or service performance) and warranty (level of reliability) of the service. This ensures that all current and planned IT Services are delivered to agreed upon and achievable service level targets

During the Service Level Management Process, the following questions are asked:
- What metrics are we collecting and comparing to?
- What utility and warranty did we promise to our customers?
- Are the targets achievable and measurable?
- Are the targets relevant?

Service Level Management is achieved through a 5-step process:
1. Negotiate
2. Agree
3. Monitor
4. Report
5. Review

Figure 16 - Service Level Management Process

It is important to always keep the Service Level Management and Business Relationship Management Process aligned as they are mutually supportive processes. Within Service Level Management, negotiation is always the key driver. Everything is open to negotiation in relations to the terms of service performance, service level targets. It is just a matter of justifying the costs associated with the parameters

Service Level Management is concerned with more than just a Service Level Agreement (SLE), the process is also responsible for the Operational Level Agreement (OLA) and the Underpinning Contract (UC)

Service Level Agreement (SLA) – is a written agreement between the IT Service Provider and the customer providing the key service targets and responsibilities of both parties. It is a formal document that is under change control, although not legally binding necessarily. It should be written in clear, concise language that is understood and agreed by both parties. It is important to monitor, report and review the SLA targets to ensure they are being achieved

Operation Level Agreement (OLA) – is an underpinning written agreement between 2 elements of a service provider organisation regarding key service targets and the responsibilities of both parties in relation to the service being supported. It is similar to an SLA but is written between internal departments within the service providers organisation

Underpinning Contract (UC) – Is a legally binding contract or agreement that conforms to law, it is written in formal legal language or "legalise" by a lawyer and is able to be held up on a court of law (if required). These contracts are negotiated and agreed upon within the Supplier Management Process

All of the SLA's, OLA's and UC's must be baselined and managed under change control, they must also be kept aligned to ensure they support the new or changed service as well as the organisational business processes. This can often be complicated as these documents can become layered in order to ensure they meet the objectives

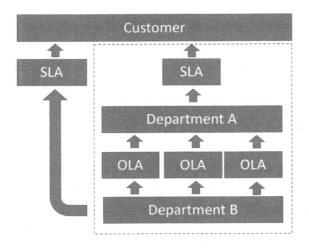

Figure 17 - SLA & OLA's

The Service Level Management Process is part of the Service Design process because t provides an ideal opportunity to establish the performance requirements early in the service deployment to ensure the design work can be directed to meet the negotiated requirements for the service

The Availability Management Process is concerned with the meeting the current and future availability needs of the business. It is responsible for ensuring that the level of availability delivered in all IT services meets the agreed needs and\or service level targets in a cost effective and timely manner

Availability – is the ability of a service, system or configuration item to perform its function, when required there are 2 types of availability:
Service Availability - is focused on the end-to-end service that is experienced by the end user or customer
Component Availability – if focused on each piece that together provides the end-to-end experience

The question of which is more important depends upon perspective!

If you're the end user of a service, you're not so concerned about the component availability, your more focused upon whether the end-to-end service is working properly when you need it to, however if you're the service provider, you are potentially more concerned with the component availability. If a component fails, there may be a loss of redundancy, but the service is still functioning which means the end user will not notice any service degradation, the service provider knows that this must be resolved as soon as possible before any further issues arise and the overall service is affected.

Capacity Management Process

The Capacity Management Process is focused upon meeting the current and future capacity and performance needs of the business by ensuring that the capacity of the IT Services and the related IT infrastructure meets the agreed capacity and performance related requirements in the most cost effective and timely manner

Capacity – is he maximum throughput of a service, system or a configuration item. Capacity planning is conducted from the top down, beginning with the business capacity management, then service capacity management, and finally to the component management

Business Capacity Management – aims at aligning capacity management to the business plans and business strategy. It translates the requirements into services and infrastructure whilst coordinating with the Business Relationship Management Process

Service Capacity Management – ensures that the services that underpin the business processes and outcomes by focusing upon the end-to-end performance of operational services and workloads. Service capacity must be coordinated and aligned to the Service Portfolio Management Process

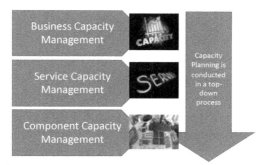

Figure 18 - Capacity Planning

Component Capacity Management – aims at ensuring that there is an appropriate level of understanding relating to the technical components within the infrastructure by employing data analysis techniques to obtain the maximum value from components. Component Capacity must be coordinated with the Configuration Management Process to ensure the optimal configuration items are used, ensuring the maximum efficiency and minimal cost associated

The Capacity Management Process is responsible for creating the capacity plan for the organization. The Capacity Plan should include the details of the current and historic utilization level and performance, a forecast of the capacity changes needed to support the future requirements, a list of assumptions used in the planning, and a costed list of recommendations for future implementation

This capacity plan is used by the Information Technology (IT) Director to make informed service decisions, the IT Director is in a constant balancing act or battle for the resources within the organisation. This is battle of supply vs demand, alongside other consideration like cost and physical resource availability. The IT Director will consider whether the current infrastructure can support new or revised services, as well as if additional infrastructure must be purchased to support any new or changed services

IT Service Continuity Management Process
The IT Service Continuity Management Process is responsible for ensuring that the service provider can provide the minimum agreed upon levels of service by managing the risks associated with a disaster or any other associated incidents that could have any impact on the ability to provide critical IT Services

Continuity management is focused upon the management of risk. Each risk is managed, and that risk management process focuses upon the likely events and their possible impacts to the IT Operations and the services provided. Continuity management focuses on the unlikely, but realistically conceivable events that could have major impacts upon the IT services. Therefore, contingency plans should be considered and made to cover these services in the unlikely event that the risk occurs.

For each event or risk analysis completed, a Business Impact Analysis (BIA) should be conducted to better understand and inform the IT Service Continuity Plan

The IT Service Continuity Management is different than the Availability Management, if an event is classified as low impact or highly likely to occur it is covered by Availability Management, for example, if there is a likelihood that a network card could fail in a server and this likelihood is classed as high, the Availability Management process should have planned to have a backup Network Card or redundant network cards installed in the server to prevent any negative impact to the services being provided

	Low Impact	High Impact
High Likelihood	Availability Management	Availability Management
Low Likelihood	Availability Management	IT Service Continuity Management

Figure 19 - Availability Management Vs Capacity Management

Instead, if we consider a high impact, low likelihood event such as a road being dug up that destroys the power lines to our Data Centre, this event would be planned for through the IT Service Continuity Management Process. In this scenario, you may plan to have offsite backups of the data or a redundant data centre that is located in a separate location that has separate power and data feeds. There are many ways to plan for a recovery solution after a disaster occurs, and these are all out of the scope of the ITIL® 2011 Foundation exam, however the idea is that a disaster is planned for under the IT Service Continuity Management Process and it is important to remember this for the exam

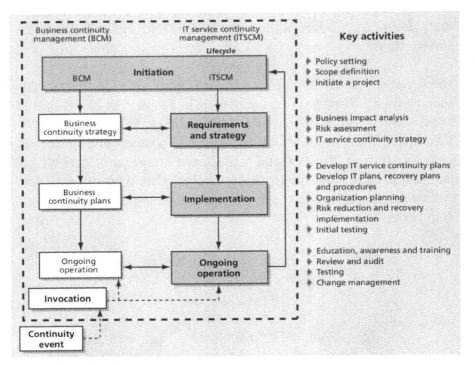

Figure 20 - Lifecycle of IT Service Continuity Management

Information Security Management Process

The Information Security Management Process aims to align the IT Security with the Business Security and to ensure that the IT Security aspects match the agreed upon needs of the business by protecting the IT assets and services from any security threats. It should align and fit into the organisations larger security management efforts.

Within this process, the IT Security Policy for the organisation is created\developed and managed\maintained. This policy is used by the Access Management Process during the Service Operation

Information Security is always focused upon the three key principles

1. Confidentiality
2. Integrity
3. Availability

Confidentiality – ensures that only those with a "need to know or access" can access the information system or data held by the system. This is most often accomplished using a mix of encryption and rights management

Integrity - ensures that the data and the services are complete, accurate and un-modified.

Availability – ensures the customer can only access the data they are authorised to access when tey need to access it

Information Systems
Security, Data &
Services

Figure 21 - Information Security

To create a secure system that has confidentiality, integrity and availability, it is a balancing act. As security increases, it becomes more difficult for users of the system to accomplish their goals and operations can suffer because of this. Just like there is a balancing act between utility and warranty, there must also be balance the security of the service against the operations of the service

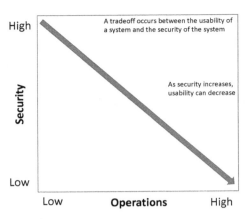

Figure 22 - Security Vs Operations

When it comes to Information Security Management, it must be remembered that while a service can be outsourced, the responsibility for the security and data protection in relation that service can never be outsourced. If a service is outsourced to a 3rd party, the contract must specify the responsibilities for the 3rd party to follow your organisation's IT security Policy.

Supplier Management Process

The Supplier Management Process is responsible for obtaining a level of service that is acceptable from the suppliers that provides a fiscal value to meet upon the agreed needs of the business and ensures suppliers meet their contractual obligations.

As the organisation spends money with 3rd part suppliers, this process attempts to ensure value is obtained for that capital investment and expense

The Supplier Management Process is similar to the Service Level Management Process but is concerned with external suppliers only instead of internal suppliers and customers. Many organisations have a heavy reliance upon external suppliers to ensure the delivery of their own services to their customers

There are four categories of suppliers
1. Strategic Suppliers
2. Operational Suppliers

3. Tactical Suppliers
4. Commodity Suppliers

Strategic Suppliers – involves the sharing of long term organisational plans between the organisation and the supplier. This is useful for example if you're a service provider who is looking at the rollout of a new Wide Area Network (WAN) allowing the supplier to understand your long-term goals and needs to support the organisation objectives

Operational Suppliers – supply the operational services such as the hosting of a data centre and data storage for the organisation

Tactical Suppliers – have a significant commercial activity with the organisation and interaction with the organisation, for example if you have a contract for the removal and storage of your daily backup tapes and the storage of your organisations critical data

Commodity Suppliers – involves the provision of low value products, for example the supply of ink cartridges or the supply of keyboards and mice for the computers

SERVICE TRANSITION PHASE

Overview

The service transition stage readies a new or changed service for operation. The primary activity done during this stage is Transition Planning and Support. This process plans all of the activities that must take place to put the service into production. This may involve the creation of a number of RFCs that will carry out all necessary changes (Change Management) and deployments (Release and Deployment Management).

Prior to moving the service into production, there may be a period of testing and validating the service to ensure sufficient quality of the service.

An overall evaluation framework is used by transition planning and support to determine if the service is still in an acceptable state to proceed or must be remediated in some manner.

As the service is readied for production, various configuration items and assets must be assembled and configured. Information about all of these CIs and assets, as well as the relationships between all of these elements, must be maintained in order to provide the best support for the service.

Knowledge about the services and underlying CIs and service as- sets is collected during this stage and subsequent stages in order to provide effective support for service faults.

Objectives

The objectives of this chapter are to enable you to:

- Describe and understand the Service Transition phase
- Describe the Service V-Model in the Service Transition Phase
- Describe quality on Service Design
- Describe the Change Management Process
- Describe the Release and Deployment Management Process
- Describe the Service Asset and Configuration Management Process

- Describe the Service Validation and Testing Process
- Describe the Transition Planning and Support Process
- Describe the Evaluation process
- Describe the Knowledge Management Process

The Service Transition phase is primarily focused upon the management of change and more specifically the introduction of new and or changed services into the live environment. During the Service Transition phase, things are actually purchased, installed, configured, tested, launched and operated

The Service Transition phase creates value to the organisation by enabling the business change whilst minimising the impact to the business through the risks associated with an unplanned or uncontrolled change. It enables the business to make use of new or changed services and ensures that the designs created within the Service Design phase are implemented as intended. During this phase, the Service Management organisation is prepared to ensure the new or changed service can be supported, the testing ad validation takes place to reduce the number of defects that are introduced into the live environment

By the completion of the Service Transition phase, the physical deployment and implementation of the new service if completed, the service is thoroughly tested and transitioned into the live environment, the configuration of the service is documented, and the operations team have been trained and are ready to support the new service

There are seven processes within the Service Transition phase:
1. Change Management
2. Release and Deployment Management
3. Service Asset and Configuration Management
4. Service Validation and Testing
5. Transition Planning and Support
6. Evaluation
7. Knowledge Management

The diagram above represents a more real world view of the ITIL Lifecycle

The Service V Model

The Service V Model defines the progressive levels of activity and the levels of testing\validation towards and defined objective, such as a release, or a major change. The testing that occurs at each level is imperative and must be complete prior to moving to the next level in order to reduce the risk during the implementation of a new or changed service

The stakeholders defined the requirements and move the service down the Service V-Model, the service provider then up the right-hand side of the model by conducting service validation and testing

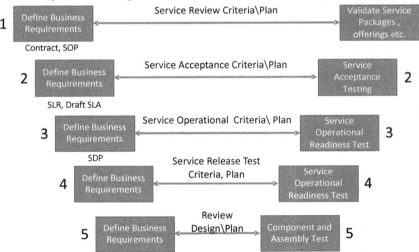

Figure 23 - Service V-Model

Change Management Process

The **Change Management Process** controls the lifecycle of all changes in order to enable beneficial changes to be made with a minimal disruption to IT Service. It is primarily concerned with recording, evaluating, approving, testing and reviewing changes to services, systems and Configuration Items (CI)

The definition of change is "the addition, modification or removal of anything that could have an effect on IT servicers"

Remember!!! All changes involve risk

To initiate a change in the Change Management Process, a Request for Change (RFC) must be submitted. An RFC is a documented request to alter, modify or remove a service or CI. RFCs are issued by customers, IT staff, users or any stakeholder and are received by the Service Desk

Once the change is submitted or initiated, it flows through a series of activities or steps including,
- The recoding of the RFC
- A review of the RFC
- Assessment and evaluation of the RFC
- Authorisation of the RFC
- Planning
- Implementation and coordination
- Review
- Closure of the RFC

Changes come in the types within ITIL® 2011
1. Normal
2. Standard
3. Emergency

Normal Change – is a change that has a uniqueness to it that represents a higher risk or uncertainty in relation to the outcome. This is the default type of change that occurs, and the assumption is that all changes are raised as a Normal Change unless stated otherwise. Emergency and standard are variations of the Normal Change procedures, an example is the introduction of a new server into the live environment
Standard Change – is a typical change that occurs on daily basis and is classed as low risk, these changes usually utilise a shorter version of the

change process or procedure and aims to minimise the bureaucracy involved in order to satisfy both the needs of the Change Management Process and also satisfy the needs of the customer, an example is the office move that occurs on a regular basis

Emergency Change – An Emergency Change addresses the unforeseen issues that occur during live operations such as failures, security threats or emergency releases to address vulnerabilities. This type of change is a rapid change that is required to ensure the business can operate. Emergency Changes should still follow the documented procedures and use the Emergency Change Management Process

All changes must be properly authorised, by the someone with the appropriate level of authority. For the ITIL® 2011 Foundation Exam, you need to be aware of the 3types of change and the 3 authorities that authorise change

1. Change Manager
2. Change Advisory Board
3. Emergency Change Advisory Board

The **Change Manager** is the effectively the protector of the standards and processes and the gate keeper to entering the live operational environment. The Change Manager is responsible for ensuring that all change authorities have approved the changes before the final decision (ideally approval) is taken. The role is to ensure food governance and to provide the final approval on all RFC's

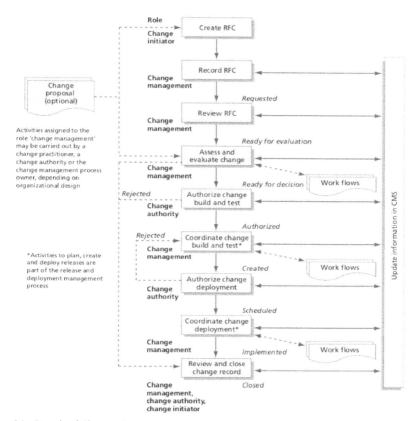

Figure 24 - Standard Change Process

The **Change Advisory Board** (CAB) is responsible for providing the Go\No-Go decision for all changes. This group meets on a regular basis and in many larger organisations there can be smaller CAB's, but one is always the final decision maker, for example you may go through a project CAB to demonstrate the project outputs are ready for transition into operations and then proceed to the main CAB for final approval before the service release

The Emergency Change Advisory Board (ECAB) is a special CAB or group convened by the Change Manager to advise upon the approval\rejection and planning for emergency changes. The membership of the ECAB includes people with the right level of experience and authority to make rapid decisions based upon an often-expedited risk-assessment.

Even after the ECAB approves the change and the change is implemented, it is important for the normal change to be revisited or reviewed to ensure that the appropriate documentation has been updated

A crucial part of the Change Management Process is the development of the change models or procedures to be used by the organisation. A Change Model is a group of defined steps, procedures and guidelines that are used to handle a certain type of change. Whilst there are numerous change models that exist, there should be only one for each CI. These change models are used to minimise the risks, save time and money and improve the consistency of executing changes within the organisation

Change models can be simple or complex, simple change models can be used for tasks like password changes or office moves, whereas complex change models should be used for tasks like new service introductions, rollouts or migrations, large scale changes to the live environment or changes that introduce significant risk to the organisation

Release and Deployment Management Process

The **Release and Deployment Management Process** is responsible for the planning, scheduling and controlling the build, test, and deployment of releases, as well as the delivery of new functionality that is required or requested by the business whilst protecting the integrity of existing services. The release and deployment schedule is based upon the technical and business criteria for the organisation

The definition of a **Release** is "one or more changes to an IT Service that are built, tested and deployed together to achieve an objective"

Each release consists of software, hardware, configurations, or a combination of these

A **Release Unit** is a particular set of configuration items released together for a specific deployment effort

Service Asset and Configuration Management

The **Service Asset and Configuration Management** (SACM) Process aims at ensuring that assets needed to deliver the services are managed and that accurate, reliable information about those services is available. Service Asset and Configuration Management is vital to the Knowledge Management Process

A major information item within the Service Asset and Configuration Management Process is the Configuration Items (CI's) CI's are the individual records within the Configuration Management Database (CMDB). Each CI is a component or service that needs to be identified and managed

A baseline in configuration management is the documented and validated configuration of a component, system or service. It is a snapshot of a particular configuration at a specific point in time (often referred to as a line in the sand) and acts as the starting point when the new equipment arrives. Any changes from the baseline must be documented to account for the differences in the services design since its operation, In Information Security, it is common to create baselines for each type of workstation or service to ensure that proper configurations are maintained, these are often referred to as Images.

The **Configuration Management System** (CMS) an essential set of tools, data and information on the configuration of the components, systems and services. It is a part of the Service Knowledge Management System (SKMS) and each SKMS can have only on definitive CMS. The CMS includes information on incidents, service requests, changes, problems, releases, errors, and any associated information

The **Definitive Media Library** (DML) is a secure storage area for the authorised software versions for every configuration item, including the licensing information and documentation. Before each item is placed into the DML it must be quality checked for integrity to ensure that there is nothing malicious that could cause any risk to the organisation

The DML can be internal or external depending upon the types of software beings stored

Service Validation and Testing Process

The **Service Validation and Testing Process** provides a separate and more focused support for testing the service, its systems and its components prior to release. By using the Service Validation and Testing process, higher levels of quality and control can and often are achieved with fewer errors entering the operational environment

Testing is performed under both the Change Management and Release & Deployment Processes. It is important to use different testers in the Service Validation and Testing process in order to ensure full compliance and validation of the service. This system of checks and balances creates a higher quality service for release.

Transition Planning and Support Process

The **Transition Planning and Support Process** provides broader support for large scale transitions and releases. If your organisation has a large volume of changes, it can often be helpful to implement this as a separate process. For example, if the organisation is about to relocate head office with all staff and services, it would be beneficial to set up a separate Transition Planning and Support process to help meet the additional business objectives more successfully and allow the normal process to continue in isolation

Evaluation Process

The **Evaluation process** provides support for post-release evaluation and confirmation of customer acceptance of the new or changed service. If your organisation has had problems with customer acceptance historically, it can be helpful to implement this as a separate process

Knowledge Management Process

The **Knowledge Management** process provides support for the capture and effective publishing of knowledge during the Service Transition phase. Knowledge Management begins in Service Transition but continues throughout the lifecycle. Knowledge Management is primarily concerned with the transition of data to information to knowledge to wisdom as known as the DIKW pyramid or model

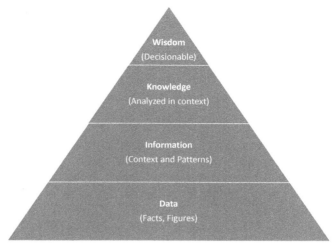

Figure 25 - DIKW Model

Data can come from many sources, such as configuration databases, service management tools, open sources, workshops, suppliers. The Service Knowledge Management System (SKMS) contains all of the data in a collection of repositories and systems. The Service Knowledge Management System also houses the Configuration Management System (CMS) and the CMS contains the Configuration Management Database (CMDB)

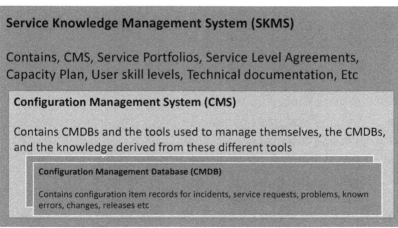

Figure 26 - Knowledge Management

SERVICE OPERATIONS PHASE

Overview

In the Service Operation stage, a service is available for IT end users. During execution of the service, it is monitored to determine service levels as well as to look for operational faults.

Operational faults may be detected as events from service monitoring. Those events may be resolved within Event Management or may be escalated to Incident Management to be resolved by Service Desk personnel. In either case, the event is recorded as an incident and the service is restored as quickly as possible via either a workaround or some other resolution.

Faults may also be detected by users, who may contact the Ser- vice Desk to log an incident. The Incident Management process is used by the Service Desk to get the service restored to the user as quickly as possible.

The Problem Management process supports the Incident Management process by looking for incident trends (problems) and resolving root causes of those problems. This process also proactively addresses any faults not yet previously identified.

The user may also contact the Service Desk to carry out simple, virtually risk-free actions (service requests) that cannot be performed by the user (Request Fulfilment) or to provide access to services or service assets (Access Management).

Objectives

The objectives of this chapter are to enable you to:

- Describe and understand the Service operations Phase
- Describe the principles of the Service Operation Phase
- Describe the Incident Management Phase
- Describe the Problem Management Process
- Describe the Event Management Process
- Describe the Service Request Fulfilment Process
- Describe the integration of Service Operations

The Service Operations phase begins upon the transition of a new or changed service to facilitate the outcomes desired by customers. All urgent operational problems are handled by this stage, whilst non-operational problems are fed back into the Service Strategy, Service Design or Service Transition as appropriate through the use of the Continual Improvement process

The Service Operations phase creates value to the organisation by ensuring that the services are operating within the expected performance parameters, restoring services quickly and efficiently in the event of a service interruption, minimizing the impact to the business in the event of a service interruption, providing a single point of focus or contact between the users of the service and the Service Provider, and by having value realised by the customer through the provision of an operational service

The Service Operations phase never really ends, it provides feedback into the earlier stages for future development of the service in future releases or revisions. During Service Operations, the Service Provider provides its users and customers with the agreed upon levels of service and attempts to meets or exceed the agreed service levels. Any faults are identified, quickly fixed where possible, or referred back to an earlier stage of the process for correction and implementation in future versions or revisions of the service

In the Service Operations phase, there are 5 process that must be learnt:
1. Incident Management
2. Problem Management
3. Event Management
4. Service Request Fulfilment
5. Access Management

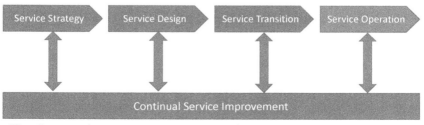

The diagram above represents a more real world view of the ITIL Lifecycle

For effective service operations to occur, the Service Provider must ensure they seek a balance and communicate with the key stakeholders

The first essential or crucial principle of Service Operations is balance, this is focused upon four areas when attempting to find the proper balance in IT:
1. Internal IT Vs external IT
2. Business stability Vs responsiveness
3. Cost Vs quality
4. Proactive Vs reactive

Each of these are a struggle for IT Service Management within the organisation, each of them represents a cost of operating a business, as well as a cost relating to a level of quality and support to the customers and users. Achieving the most optimal balance to maximise the value to the customer whilst minimising the cost to the service provider is the continual challenge of IT Service Management

The second essential principle is communication. Communication is critical component of IT Operations and key element of any successful IT Operations. Whether the communication is between the Service Provider and the users\customers, or between operations teams\shifts, there can never be enough communication within the IT Service Management organisation. Communication with leadership through the performance reporting enables the leadership to make better decisions through the provision of knowledge

Within any given project or program, communication in relation to issues early can save time and money in the longer term. Anytime a change, release or deployment is planned it must be communicated with both the end users and the support teams to avoid a n unnecessary influx of tickets or service calls. Finally, when things go wrong (and they will) communicate the status of failures, exceptions, and emergencies to ensure that both the customers and users know the status and when the issue is expected to be resolved

Incident Management Process

The **Incident Management Process** is responsible for restoring normal service operation as quickly as possible whilst minimising the impacts upon business operations, ensuring that the agreed upon levels of service quality are maintained for the customer or users. This covers any event or occurrence that disrupts or may disrupt service delivery

The definition of an **Incident** "is an unplanned interruption to an IT Service, a reduction in the quality of an IT Service, or failure of a CI that may impact a service"

The definition of an **Event** "is any change of state of an infrastructure or other item which has significance for the delivery of the service"

The definition of a **Problem** "is the underlying cause of one or more incident, or even possible incidents (such as a warning)"

The definition of a **Workaround** "is a method to minimise or eliminate the impact of an incident until a permanent fix can be implemented"

The definition of a **Known Error** "is a problem that has a documented root cause and a workaround exists (Documented means recorded). It is not as good a permanent solution, but it allows the business operations to continue until a permanent solution can be developed and implemented.

Every known error is stored in the **Known Error Database** (KEDB). This database forms part of the Configuration Management System (CMS) and details problems workarounds and known errors in a common database. It contains error records and problem records for ease of searching and researching of issues

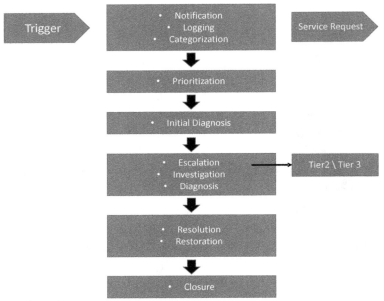

Figure 27 - Incident Management Process

Detection\Identification occurs when a trigger happens, such as an exception in the event Management Process, a technician discovers am issue, the system auto-detects an issue and creates a service ticket, or a user calls to complain about an issue

Logging occurs by the Service Desk for all incidents. The Help-Desk Analysts create a service ticket with as much information as they can gather in relation to the incident

Classification\Categorisation is performed by the Service Desk. Based upon the categorisation, the Service Ticket is then pushed to the Service Request Process or is treated as an incident per the Incident Management Process in accordance with the Service Level Agreement

Next the incident itself is prioritised based upon triage of events and priority. The impact is determined based upon the effect to the business and the urgency is assessed based upon how long before the impact is considered significant. Prioritisation is based upon the Service Level Agreement, which determines the timeline to identify and resolve an incident.

Priority	Category	Time to correct
1	Critical	1 hour
2	High	2 hours
3	Medium	36 hours
4	Low	72 hours
5	When able	N\A

Figure 28 - incident Prioritisation Matrix

During the initial Diagnosis and Escalation, Tier 1 support performs initial triage on the incident asking, Can I fix this quickly, Do I need specialist. Based upon the answers to those questions, the Service Desk will either fix the issue or escalate to a higher tier of support specialist (Tier 2 or Tier 3)

There are 2 forms of escalation:

Functional Escalation – is the most common type of escalation and occurs when an incident requires specialist skills or skills beyond the initial tier of Service Desk Support

Hierarchical Escalation - occurs when an incident is referred to management due to the severity of the incident, the person affected by the incident or the need for special permission to obtain replacement components due to a cost threshold that has been created by the incident,

Even though the incident may be escalated, the Service Desk still owns the incident throughout its entire lifecycle

Resolution and Recovery occurs once the investigation is complete and appropriate incident correction occurs. The solution to the incident is reported back to the Service Desk and the affected user

Finally, the closure of the incident occurs, however the Service Desk do not take the word of the technician. The Service Desk will first contact the end user who raised the incident and verify that the fix\resolution have corrected the issue, if this is the case, then the incident ticket can be closed and the details of the original incident, the resolution\fix will be documented thoroughly within the incident ticket

Problem Management Process

The **Event Management Process** works to manage the change of state that has significance for the management of a CI or a Service throughout its lifecycle. The lifecycle of an event is usually very short, there are 3 types of events –

1. Informational events
2. Warning events
3. Exception events

Informational Events – are usually indicated as green and highlights that everything is operating as expected.

Warning Events – are usually indicated as a yellow and is indicating that something is not operating as expected

Exception Events – are usually indicated as red and are indicating that an error has occurred, it is indicating that a level of performance is unacceptable

Service Request Fulfilment Process

The Service Request Fulfilment Process manages the lifecycle for all service requests from all users and delivers value directly and swiftly to the users by enhancing their efficiency and effectiveness. This process also assists users in situations where no service degradation or service interruption is involved

Often users will try to circumvent the Service Request Fulfilment Process, as tempting as it is to try and help users, especially when they approach you directly. It shouldn't be done, in most circumstances when the users bypass the process, the resolution takes longer, and the user will only become aggravated, as will the IT Staff involved. Follow the process, it works!

The Service Request Fulfilment Process is responsible for different types of requests, for example the creation of user accounts, procurement and installation of new hardware or software, resetting passwords, desk moves etc

Every request should be recorded in the Service Knowledge management System, as this can and will help in the Continual Service Improvement Process, each Service Request can trigger other processes, for example the Change Management Process, Incident Management Process or the Problem Management Process

It is worth remembering that the Service Request Fulfilment Process is about handling all requests, but not necessarily solving them for the users. Some requests are simply not possible to fulfil, regardless the request is submitted into the system and the process is followed before a rejection is issued to the user

Access Management Process
The Access Management Process provides the rights to allow the right users to the access the data or service they have the permission to access. The Access Management Process simply executes the IT Security Policy as defined by the organisation during the Information Security Management Process

Some organisations don't treat access management as a separate process and combine this into the Service Request Fulfilment Process, Change Management or Release and Deployment Process dependent upon the organisations design

Integration of Service Operations
As already explained, many of the Service Operation Processes are tightly integrated, for example the Event Management Process can trigger the Problem Management Process, or a Service Request can trigger the Incident Management Process. Each of the process is interwoven together by events, incidents or problems which form the core of the Service Operations phase workload

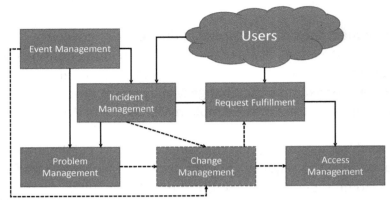

Figure 29 - Process Integration

Whilst it looks like a chart of random connections or spaghetti, however if you consider some examples which we will highlight how this would work in the real world to explain these connections

Firstly, notice the dashed lines within Figure 29, these represent process outside the Service Operation Phase, but still have ties into the Service Operations Phase. Change Management for example is a process within the Service Transition Phase, but still receives inputs from the Service Operations Processes and provides them as inputs as well

A typical scenario in the real world, A user calls the Service Desk with an issue that then creates an incident. The incident is found to be more systematic which then means it is categorised as a problem. This problem then creates a workaround, becoming a known error and eventually, the solution is designed. To implement the identified solution a change request is raised and once fielded, the problem is resolved and closed

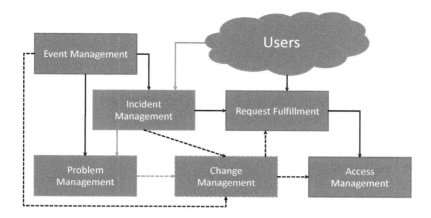

As you can see, the process are highly integrated, in the next example consider that the IT Operations function has noticed a large number of users are having issues logging into the a service. The IT Operations team recommends that a problem is created. Once a solution is determined, they recommend a change through the Change Management Process, which will ultimately require changes to the access rights for a particular set of users, which is ultimately implemented by the Access Management Process

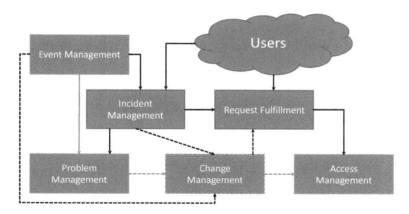

Once the Service is in the Service Operations Phase, each process and function works together to provide the end users (customers) with successful and efficient services

CONTINUAL SERVICE IMPROVEMENT

Overview

During the Continual Service Improvement stage, the IT organisation collects data and feedback from users, customers, stake- holders, and other sources to enhance services and how they are provided.

This involves the use of a seven-step improvement process that collects data, analyses the data, provides recommendations, and implements those recommendations.

In support of the improvement process, Service Level Management collects information from IT users and customers and data from the operation of the services. Service measurement and re- porting provides standard vehicles for describing the performance of the services.

Finally, all service improvements must be scrutinized according to whether they meet the needs of the business and provide an overall return on investment.

Objectives

The objectives of this chapter are to enable you to:

- Describe and understand the Continual Service Improvement Phase
- Describe measurements and metrics
- Describe the 7-Step Process Improvement Process
- Describe the Deming Cycle
- Describe the Continual Service Improvement Model
- Describe the role of automation in ITIL® 2011

The Continual Service Improvement Phase focuses upon the alignment and realignment of services, processes and functions to the changing needs of the business. While it is most useful starting the Service Operations Phase, it does occur throughout all of the stages of the ITIL® 2011 Lifecycle. By performing a strenuous Continual Service Improvement Phase, the IT Service Management organisation can identify those processes and functions that need to be strengthened to increase efficiency

The Continual Service Improvement Phase creates value to the business by ensuring services, processes and other aspects of service management are aligned with business objectives, that the services meet the agreed upon performance levels, that the efficiency of service delivery is always improving by minimising cost, and that all aspects of service management are undergoing constant reviews

The main objective or goal of the Continual Service Improvement Phase is to increase efficiency. This is done by:
- Tracking customer issues,
- Determining what issues keep occurring,
- Determining processes are failing
- What service agreements aren't working

All relevant information must be captured to inform appropriate actions to fix the identified areas of improvement by feeding back into earlier phases of the ITIL® 2011 lifecycle. Each inter-process link is verified as functional, effective and efficient. Measurement and metrics are essential to performing Continual Service Improvement well, especially gathering and analysing the service operations data

The primary output of this phase is the Service Improvement Plan (SIP). The **Service Improvement Plan** (SIP) maps specific improvement objectives for an identified time period between service reviews. The Continual Service Improvement phase never really ends, in essence you could actually do Continual Service Improvement upon the Continual Service Improvement phase!

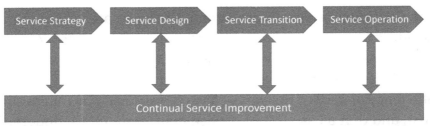

The diagram above represents a more real world view of the ITIL Lifecycle

Within the Continual Service Improvement Phase, there is effectively only one process needed for the ITIL® 2011 Foundation exam, The 7-Step Process Improvement Process

Measurements & Metrics
In order to improve any service or process, it is important to have a clear method to quantifiably measure the success or failures. Measurements are useful to validate previous managerial decisions by providing evidence that services are being correctly performed through the provision of evidence

Additionally, they can be used to direct activities by setting targets and determining of the Service Level Agreement (SLA) targets are being met or exceeded. When a particular course of action is up for decision, measurements can provide evidence that a certain path is the correct one based upon the facts and figures.

Finally, measurements can be used to determine when an error needs to be corrected. For example, metrics and measurements can be useful to determine when a threshold is breached through Event Management and an incident or problem needs to be initiated.

These four reasons for measurement can be summarised as Justify, Direct, Validate and Intervene

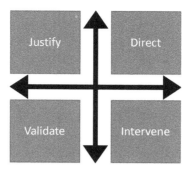

It is a simple fact, that Senior Management and decision makers love metrics and pretty pictures, the higher up the organisational ladder they go the more pictures they like!

Metrics are a measure that is captured and reported on for a given process, service or activity

There are 3 types of metrics within ITIL® 2011
1. Technology Metrics
2. Process Metrics
3. Service Metrics

Technology Metrics – measure components or application-based measurements, for example server availability or network availability
Process Metrics – measures the process workflow through the use of management tools
Service Metrics – measures an end-to-end experience of a service through the use of management tools

Metrics are a baseline of measurement that is used within IT Service Management. These metrics become Key Performance Indicators (KPIs). A **Key Performance Indicator** (KPI) is a metric used to help manage an IT service, process or activity and is supported by metrics. KPIs can be either quantitative (measuring the amount of something) or qualitative (measuring the quality of something). The KPI is then rolled up into a Critical Success Factor (CSF)

The **Critical Success Factor** (CSF) is something that must happen for a service, process or activity to succeed in its objectives. CSFs are supported by related KPIs

The objective establishes the reason for measurement in the first place. Measurements themselves have no value on its own, its only value is to support the achievement of a specific objective

For example, the provision of email services during core business hours (0800-1700hrs) – which is the objective. It could be measured using the using the CSF that the Exchange Server and the associated services must be available between the hours of 0730-1730

The CSF is fed by one or more KPIs, such as maintaining a 99.99% uptime for the MS Exchange Server, this KPI could be fed by multiple metrics, for example – Server uptime, network availability, External email access uptime etc

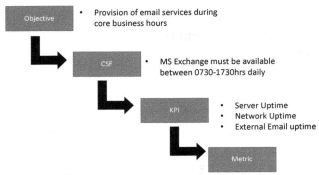

Figure 30 - Measuring Objectives

The 7-Step Process Improvement Process
The 7-Step Process Improvement Process forms the core of the Continual Improvement Phase within the ITIL® 2011 lifecycle.

The 7-Step Process Improvement Process consists of:
1. Define the vision\strategy
2. Define what is to be measured
3. Gather the relevant data
4. Process the data for analysis – so that that data becomes information
5. Analyse the data for trends so the information becomes knowledge
6. Leaders assess knowledge and produce Service Improvement Plans (SIPs)

7. Implement the agreed upon changes

Deming Cycle

While the ITIL® 2011 Foundation exam requires that you memorise the 7-Step Process Improvement Process steps, it also expects you to understand the Deming Cycle, which heavily influences the 7-Step Process Improvement Process's development

The Deming Cycle is an improvement model developed by W Edward Deming and has found great success in the Japanese auto manufacturing industry. The Deming Cycle is fairly simple, it has only 4 steps:
1. Plan
2. Do
3. Check
4. Act

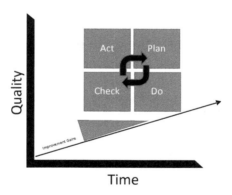

The Deming Cycle side by side against the ITIL® 2011 7-Step Process Improvement Process shows just how aligned they are and fit into each other

Deming	Step	Activity
Plan	1 2	• Identify Vision, Strategy, Goals • Define what to measure
Do	3 4	• Gather data • Process data
Check	5 6	• Analyse data • Present and use information
Act	7	• Implement changes

Figure 31 - Deming Vs 7-Step Process Improvement Process

The final improvement model covered by the ITIL® 2011 Foundation Exam is called the Continual Service Improvement Model. This model is a simple set of guiding questions to organise and perpetuate an improvement program within a service management organisation. It also closely mirrors or is aligned to the ITIL® 2011 7-Step Process Improvement Process

This model begins with the question, what is the vision? and ends with the question How do we keep the momentum? at which point the process repeats the cycle by asking the questions again in an effort to continually improve the service

Role of automation in ITIL

It's a simple fact, we as human beings can only focus on a limited number of things at once when we need to make a decision in complex situations. This is called bounded rationality, because of this limitation, automation is extremely important to help us to understand the wide array of factors that affect service management better

Automation is used to identify patterns and trends in large data sets, for example within event logs, incident logs, service desk logs, change requests. Through the use of automation, making decisions can effectively be simplified for those decision makers allowing them to view complex scenarios, analyse large amounts of information or data and make the best decision

Automation can also aid in the guarantee of constancy in relation to the data and during the design phases of the lifecycle, through the utilisation of toolsets like design software or modelling and simulation software.

Automation can also support ITIL through the accurate recording of large volumes of data such as incident logs, event logs, exchange server transaction logs. Whilst computers are basically designed to handle large volumes of data, people make mistakes when compiling large volumes of data from differing sources.

Finally, automation is almost a necessity if the service management organisation wishes to achieve anything close or that represents real time response's and reporting in relation to issues or events. The simple truth is that there is simply too much data coming from too many sources for a person to be able to make sense of let alone be able to actually review and make a decision in a timely manner, however if the organisation uses automation in relation to problems, incidents and logs, these can all be combined, and the issues responded to in near real-time

It is important to consider how and what to automate, your organisation should always try to remember to define the processes accurately before any attempts are made to buy and apply any automation solution. Each process should be as simple as possible before attempting to automate the process or processes. Efficiency is important in relation to your processes, your automation will simply not be effective or do the wrong thing , but do it wrong more effectively and quickly

CONCLUSION
OBJECTIVES

The objective of this chapter is to prepare you to take the exam and provide study hints or tips

At this point, we have covered everything you need to know in order to take and successfully pass the (ITIL®) 2011 Foundations exam. If you have ready and understood everything you have read so far, you are almost ready to sit for the exam with confidence and to pass it on your first attempt!

W covered all the essentials you need to know, with no fluff, filler, or extra material, and hopefully you have been able to read and learn the material quickly and are getting ready to conquer the certification exam

The next piece of the book contains a full-length practice certification exam.

The practice exam is 40 questions long, just like the real exam. To get the maximum benefit from these exams, I recommend you find a quiet place to take them and time yourself for 60 minutes (just like the real exam).

Once you finish each exam, you will find all the answers and explanations listed after each exam.

It is important to take the time to go over each question and answer. If you missed a question, review the explanation and ensure you understand why it is the correct answer.

If you have read this entire book and took both practice exams scoring at least an 85% or higher, you will be ready to take and pass the ITIL® 2011 Foundations exam on your first attempt!

Question Booklet

Multiple Choice
Examination Duration: 60 minutes

Instructions

1. You should attempt all 40 questions. Each question is worth one mark.
2. There is only one correct answer per question.
3. The pass mark for this exam is 26 out of 40 (65%).
4. Mark your answers on the answer sheet provided. Use a pencil (NOT pen).
5. You have 60 minutes to complete this exam.
6. This is a 'closed book' exam. No material other than the exam paper is allowed.

1. Which is NOT a source of best practice?
   a. Standards
   b. Technology
   c. Academic research
   d. Internal experience

2. Which three are the characteristics of ITIL guidance that help to make it successful?
   a. Prescriptive, best practice and solution specific
   b. Publicly available, prescriptive and best practice
   c. Vendor neutral, non-prescriptive and best practice
   d. Publicly available, solution specific and vendor neutral

3. What is the ITIL term for customers of an IT service provider who purchase services as agreed in a legal contract?
   a. Strategic customers
   b. External customers
   c. Valued customers
   d. Internal customers

4. Which is NOT defined as part of every process?
   a. Roles
   b. Inputs and outputs
   c. Functions
   d. Metrics

5. In which areas would ITIL complementary guidance provide assistance?
   a. Adapting best practice for specific industry sectors
   b. Creating service application interfaces
   c. Specialized practices for IT recruitment
   d. Integrating ITIL with other operating models

   1 and 2
   2 and 3
   3 and 4
   1 and 4

6. Which is an objective of service transition?
   a. To negotiate service levels for new services
   b. To ensure that service changes create the expected business value
   c. To reduce the impact of business-critical service outages on key services
   d. To plan and manage entries in the service catalogue

7. Which lifecycle stage ensures that the impact of service outages is minimized on a day-to-day basis?
    a. Service design
    b. Service operation
    c. Continual service improvement
    d. Service transition

8. Which is the BEST description of a service catalogue?
    a. A document used by IT staff to identify activities that must be performed
    b. A list of all service level agreements (SLAs)
    c. A list of all business requirements that have not yet become services
    d. The part of the service portfolio that is visible to customers

9. Which of the following is concerned with policy and direction?
    a. Capacity management
    b. Governance
    c. Service design
    d. Service level management

10. Which is an example of an operational level agreement (OLA)?
    a. A document that outlines agreements between service providers in the same organization
    b. A document that outlines the responsibilities of both the IT service provider and the customer
    c. A document that describes to a customer how services will be operated on a day-to-day basis
    d. A document that describes business services and their service level targets to operational staff

11. A known error record has been created after completing diagnosis of a problem but before finding a workaround.

    Is this a valid approach?
    a. Yes: a known error record can be created at any time it is prudent to do so
    b. No: a known error record should be created before the problem is logged
    c. No: a known error record is created when the original incident is raised
    d. No: a known error record should be created with the next release of the service

12. Which is used to communicate a high-level description of a major change that involved significant cost and risk to the organization?
    a. Change proposal
    b. Change policy
    c. Service request
    d. Risk register

13. Which person or group is responsible for agreeing service targets with the service provider?
    a. The user
    b. The customer
    c. The supplier
    d. The service desk staff

14. Which of the following is TRUE regarding value?
    a. Value is defined by the customer
    b. Value is defined by the cost of the service
    c. Value is determined by the features offered to the customer
    d. Value is determined in financial terms only

15. Services and technology are examples of which of the four Ps?
    a. Processes
    b. Performance
    c. Products
    d. Partners

16. What is the MAIN reason for a service provider to understand the five aspects of service design?
    a. To prevent security breaches in mission critical services
    b. To ensure a holistic, results-driven approach
    c. To allow service design to cut costs
    d. To prevent breaches of service level agreements (SLAs)

17. Which is the CORRECT set of steps in the Continual Service Improvement (CSI) approach?
    a. Devise a strategy; Design the solution; Transition into production; Operate the solution; Continually improve
    b. 'Where do we want to be?'; 'How do we get there?'; 'Who plans the improvement?'; 'How do we know we arrived?'; 'How do we keep the momentum going?'
    c. Identify the required business outcomes; Plan how to achieve the outcomes; Implement the plan; Check the plan has been properly implemented; Improve the solution
    d. 'What is the vision?'; 'Where are we now?'; 'Where do we want to be?'; 'How do we get there?'; 'Did we get there?'; 'How do we keep the momentum going?'

18. Which three types of metric support Continual Service Improvement (CSI) activities?
    a. Technology metrics, service desk metrics and Key Performance Indicator (KPI) metrics
    b. Process metrics, software metrics and financial metrics
    c. Technology metrics, process metrics and service metrics
    d. Service metrics, technology metrics and Key Performance Indicator (KPI) metrics

19. Which part of Financial Management for IT services deals with predicting and controlling income and expenditure within the organization?
    a. Accounting
    b. Budgeting
    c. Cost models
    d. Charging

20. What is the PRIMARY process for strategic communication with the service provider's customers?
    a. Service catalogue management
    b. Service portfolio management
    c. Service desk
    d. Business relationship management

21. Which of these recommendations are best practice for service level agreements?
    a. Include legal terminology in service level agreements (SLAs)
    b. Ensure all the targets in an SLA are measurable.
    c. Ensure the SLA is signed by both customer and provider
    d. Include the service hours and cost of delivering the service

    1 and 2
    2 and 3
    3 and 4
    1 and 4

22. Which is the BEST description of a service-based service level agreement (SLA)?
    a. An agreement with an individual customer group, covering all the services that they use
    b. An agreement that covers one service for a single customer
    c. An agreement that covers service-specific issues in a multi-level SLA structure
    d. An agreement that covers one service for all customers of that service

23. Which is NOT a responsibility of service catalogue management?
    a. Ensuring that information about live IT services is accurate
    b. Ensuring that service level agreements are maintained
    c. Ensuring that information in the service catalogue is consistent with the service portfolio
    d. Ensuring that all operational services are recorded in the service catalogue

24. Which is NOT an objective of supplier management?
    a. Maintaining the supplier policy
    b. Supplier categorization and risk assessment
    c. Maintaining the service knowledge management system
    d. Identifying opportunities for the continual service improvement register

25. Which process has the objective: "To ensure all service models conform to strategic, architectural, governance, and other corporate requirements"?
    a. Service portfolio management
    b. Design coordination
    c. Service level management
    d. Change management

26. Which statement about the emergency change advisory board (ECAB) is CORRECT?
    a. The ECAB considers every high priority request for change
    b. The review of completed emergency changes is one of the duties of the ECAB
    c. The ECAB will be used for emergency changes where there may not be time to call a full CAB
    d. The ECAB will be used when a full CAB has a large backlog of changes

27. Who normally chairs a change advisory board (CAB)?
    a. Change manager
    b. Service owner
    c. Change initiator
    d. Business relationship manager

28. What is the second phase in release and deployment management?
    a. Review and close
    b. Authorize changes
    c. Release build and test
    d. Release and deployment planning

29. Which process has the objective: "to improve the quality of management decision making by ensuring that reliable and secure information is available throughout the lifecycle"?
    a. Knowledge management
    b. Availability management
    c. Service asset and configuration management
    d. Change management

30. Which process helps to ensure that new or changed services are established in supported environments within the predicted cost, quality and time estimates?
    a. Financial management for IT Services
    b. Capacity management
    c. Transition planning and support
    d. Change management

31. Which should be done when closing an incident?
    a. Check the incident categorization and correct it if necessary
    b. Check that the user is satisfied with the outcome
    c. Record a known error record with the resolution
    d. Perform an incident review for lessons learned

    1 and 2
    2 and 3
    3 and 4
    1 and 4

32. Which BEST describes hierarchic escalation?
    a. Notifying more senior levels of management about an incident
    b. Passing an incident to people with a greater level of technical skill
    c. Using more senior specialists than necessary to resolve an incident to maintain customer satisfaction
    d. Failing to meet the incident resolution times specified in a service level agreement

33. A significant, unresolved problem is likely to cause major business disruption. Where is this MOST LIKELY to be escalated to?
    a. IT service continuity management
    b. Availability management
    c. Incident management
    d. Change management

34. Which process will regularly analyse incident data to identify discernible trends?
    a. Service level management
    b. Problem management
    c. Change management
    d. Event management

35. Which is the BEST description of a service request?
    a. A request from a user for information, advice or for a standard change
    b. Anything that the customer wants and is prepared to pay for
    c. Any request or demand that is entered by a user via a self-help web-based interface
    d. Any request for change (RFC) that is low-risk and which can be approved by the change
    e. manager without a change advisory board (CAB) meeting

36. Which service desk organizational structure is NOT described in 'Service Operation'?
    a. Local service desk
    b. IT help desk
    c. Virtual service desk
    d. Follow the sun

37. Which function, or process would provide staff to monitor events in an operations bridge?
    a. Technical management
    b. IT operations management
    c. Request fulfilment
    d. Applications management

38. What is a process owner NOT responsible for?
    a. Defining the process strategy
    b. Communication of process information or changes to ensure awareness
    c. Developing IT plans that meet and continue to meet the IT requirements of the business
    d. Identifying improvement opportunities for inclusion in the CSI register

39. What is the role of a person if they are categorized as "I" in a RACI matrix?
    a. They are accountable for the outcome of the activity
    b. They must perform an activity
    c. They must be kept up to date on the progress of an activity
    d. They manage an activity

40. Which of these can be introduced to provide; improved detection and monitoring, pattern recognition analysis and service optimization?
    a. Service automation
    b. The DIKW structure
    c. Demand management
    d. Standard changes

ITIL® Foundation Examination Answers and Rationales

Q	A	Book Ref	Rationale
1	B	SS 2.1.7 Best practices in the public domain	Technology (answer B) is an enabler of best practice, not a source of best practice. Standards (answer A), academic research (answer C) and internal experience (answer D) are all sources of best practice.
2	C	SS 1.4 Why is ITIL so successful?	The guidance states that the characteristics in answer C are what contribute to ITIL's success: vendor neutral, non-prescriptive and best practice. The characteristics 'prescriptive' and 'solution specific' conflict with those that contribute to ITIL's success. 'Publicly available' is a characteristic of ITIL but is not paired with two other correct characteristics.
3	B	SS 3.2.1.2 Internal & external customers	If there is a contract, the customer must be external as contracts are not needed when the customer is internal. For this reason, internal customers (answer D) is incorrect. Strategic customers (answer A) and valued customers (answer C) may be internal or external and so may, or may not, require a contract.
4	C	SS 2.2.2 Processes	Functions are not part of a process, they carry out processes. The roles (answer A) involved in a process are always defined, even if these are only those of the process owner and process manager. No process could operate without inputs (answer B). Every process needs to be measured by metrics (answer D) to allow it to be managed effectively.
5	D	SS 1 Introduction	Only options 1 and 4 are true. The ITIL complementary guidance includes many books, blogs and white papers which describe its interface with other operating models e.g. SIAM, COBIT, etc. It also includes books and papers pertaining to specific industry sectors e.g. government, finance, etc.

			Developing application interfaces and IT recruitment would be more specific to software development and HR practices and methodologies than being complimentary to ITIL.
6	B	ST 1.1.1 Purpose and objectives of service transition	A number of service transition processes e.g. change management, help to ensure that service changes create the expected business value. The other answers are incorrect because they are objectives of processes in other lifecycle stages. Answer A is an objective of service level management. Answer C is more an objective of service operation and answer D belongs to service catalogue management.
7	B	SO 1.1.1 Purpose and objectives of service operation	As part of service operation, incident and problem management can help to minimize outages. The other answers are incorrect because they are not involved in the day-to-day running of the service: service design (answer A) creates the blueprint for the service, service transition (answer D) ensures the service moves into the live environment, and continual service improvement (answer C) helps the organization to identify areas for improvement in terms of the service's overall effectiveness and efficiency.
8	D	SS 4.2.4.5 Service catalogue structure	The service portfolio comprises the service catalogue (visible to customers) and the service pipeline and retired services (not visible to customers). Answer A is incorrect as the service catalogue sets out the description of a service not the activities that need to be carried out. Answer B is incorrect as the service catalogue is used as a basis for creating SLAs, however they are not listed within the catalogue. Answer C is incorrect as the service catalogue

			contains the services provided, and not the services required.
9	B	SS 2.3.1 Governance	Answer B is correct as Governance is solely concerned with policy and direction for the organization. Though it could be argued that the other options do have policies and set direction, but these are NOT their primary focus and they will all be driven by organizational governance standards.
10	A	SD 4.3.4 Policies, principles and basic concepts	An OLA is an agreement between an IT service provider and another part of the same organization that assists with the provision of services. Answer B describes a contract. Answer C describes information that would be found in an SLA. The description of business services in answer D is likely to be found in the service catalogue.
11	A	SO 4.4.5.7 Raising a known error record	(NB. This question concerns a 'known error record', not a 'known error'.) In some cases, it may be advantageous to raise a known error record even earlier in the overall process, even though the diagnosis may not be complete, or a workaround found. This might be used for information purposes or to identify a root cause or workaround that appears to address the problem but hasn't been fully confirmed Answer B is incorrect because although known error records can be created from external sources before a problem is logged, this is not always the case. Answer C is incorrect as a known error record would not be created from an incident record. Answer D is incorrect as the next release of the service may introduce a

			fix for the known error, making it redundant.
12	A	ST 4.2.4.6 Change proposals	A change proposal would be used where a major cost and/or risk is involved, often requiring approval from senior customer and service provider representatives. A change policy (answer B) defines when change proposals or requests should be raised. A service request (answer C) is raised for more minor levels of change, with known risks and costs. A risk register (answer D) records the nature and level of risk of events that may affect the service (that, if they occur, may necessitate changes).
13	B	SS 2.1.5 Stakeholders in service management	The customer agrees the service targets with the service provider through the SLA. Supplier (answer C) agreements are laid down in contracts. The user (answer A) of a service may not necessarily be the customer. In this case the customer would agree the targets for the service that the user will receive. The service desk staff (answer D) might be involved in reporting on targets but not in agreeing them.
14	A	SS 3.2.3.1 Creating value	The correct answer is A, value is always determined by the customer. This is because the customer's perception influences how value is measured. This is not only measured in financial terms. It is not always related to the cost of a service, or the advertised features offered.
15	C	SD 3.1.5 Comprehensive and integrated service design Fig 3.3	The correct answer is C, services and technology are examples of PRODUCTS, not partners or processes. Performance is not one of the 4 P's.

16	B	SD 3.1.1 Holistic service design	The key to the answer is the holistic nature of service design and the desire to achieve the results and create the value defined in service strategy. The other three answers are all areas that service design is concerned with, but they are not the MAIN reason.
17	D	CSI 3.1.1 Business questions for CSI	Answer D describes the complete continual service improvement approach. Answer B misses two of the steps of the approach and terms are incorrect. Answer A describes the service lifecycle, not steps in CSI. Answer C is closer to describing the Deming Cycle of 'plan, do, check, act', and again are not recognized steps in the CSI approach.
18	C	CSI 5.5 Metric	Technology, process and service are the three types of metrics that support CSI activities, as stated in the CSI publication.
19	B	SS 4.3.2 Scope	Budgeting involves looking into the future to predict expenditure and income. Accounting (answer A) is the process of recording and accounting for spending. Cost models (answer C) are used to calculate the cost of providing services. Charging (answer D) is the process through which costs can be recovered from customers.
20	D	SS 4.5.1 Purpose & objectives	Business relationship management covers communication at a strategic level. Service desk (answer C) is not a process, even though it provides service level data for reporting. Although the outputs of service portfolio management (answer B) and service catalogue management (answer A) are used in communication with the customer, they are not the process responsible for it.

21	B	SD 4.3.5.1 Designing SLA frameworks	B is the CORRECT answer. Option 1 (incorrect) - Legal terminology may be included if the SLA is part of a contract, however if the document is not legally binding, legal terminology is not necessary. Option 2 (correct) - All SLA targets must be measurable to prevent disagreements over whether they have been met. Option 3 (correct) - Both customer and provider must sign to show that they agree to their responsibilities as outlined in the SLA. SD 4.3.1, 4.3.2 Option 4 (incorrect) - The price of the service may be included, but the cost of delivering the service will not be included.
22	D	SD 4.3.5.1 Designing SLA frameworks	A service-based SLA describes the agreed level of service for a particular service, which may be provided to a number of customers. Answer A describes a customer-based SLA where a single customer has an SLA for multiple services. Answer B is half right because it covers a single service but still incorrect as it fails to identify multiple customers. Answer C describes one of the levels (the service level) of a multi-level SLA.
23	B	SD 4.2.1 Purpose & objectives	Answer B is correct as it identifies a responsibility of service level management NOT service catalogue management. The accuracy of the catalogue (answer A), consistency with the other elements of the service portfolio (answer C) and completeness of the service catalogue (answer D) are all incorrect because they are elements of service catalogue management.
24	C	SD 4.8.1 & 4.8.2 Purpose & objectives	The correct answer is C. Supplier management maintains the SCMIS, not the SKMS. The other options are valid objectives of the supplier management process.

25	B	SD 4.1.1 Purpose & objectives	The correct answer is B) Design coordination. Ensuring that the service model designs conform to requirements, including strategic, architectural, governance and corporate, is a stated objective of design coordination. Answer A – Service Portfolio Management would be concerned with controlling what services are offered, ensuring an acceptable level of return on investments, and how services are enabled to meet a business strategy. Answer C – Service level management would be concerned with establishing the relevant service performance targets and then tracking the model's conformance to service levels, once in operation. Answer D Change management would be concerned with implementing any changes to the service model and its initial implementation as part of the service transition stage of the lifecycle.
26	C	ST 4.2.5.11 Emergency changes	ITIL guidance states that the full CAB is the best body to consider a change. The ECAB will substitute if this proves logistically impossible. Answer A is incorrect as the CAB will consider some of the high priority changes where time allows to bring it together. Answer B is incorrect as the review of changes is the role of the full CAB. Answer D is incorrect an ECAB would not be used to alleviate a backlog of changes.
27	A	ST 4.2.5.10 Change advisory board	The change manager normally chairs the CAB. It is likely that the other three may attend the CAB to either contribute or take away information.
28	C	ST 4.4.5 Process activities, methods and techniques	'Release build and test' follows release and deployment planning (answer D)

			as the second phase. 'Review and close' (answer A) is the fourth and final stage. 'Change authorization' (answer B) is a change management activity and outside of the scope of release and deployment management.
29	A	ST 4.7.1 Purpose & objectives	Even though knowledge management is a process within service transition, it is described as a whole lifecycle process ensuring that reliable and secure knowledge, information and data is available and current throughout the five stages.
30	C	ST 4.1.2 Scope	Transition planning and support acts like the glue binding together the service transition stage. It would therefore be responsible for the planning and coordinating the resources required for service transitions.
31	A	SO 4.2.5.9 Process activities, methods and techniques	Options 1 and 2 are correct. The closing category of an incident should be checked as it is the raw data that can be used for many purposes, e.g. to help problem management identify trends of recurring incidents. The user must also be satisfied with the outcome as they are the people affected. This is very often done by a service desk contacting them to confirm closure.
32	A	SO 4.2.5.6 Incident escalation	Hierarchic escalation takes place if a higher-level authority needs to be informed and/or make a decision, often to focus attention on an incident resolution. Answers B and C describe functional escalation but not escalation up the hierarchy of the organization. Answer D is a reason that hierarchic escalation may be carried out, but it is not a description of it.
33	A	SO 4.4.6.4 Interfaces	If business disruption is likely, then continuity management must assess

			the situation and decide how to act. Availability management (answer B) is more focused on design activity. Incident management (answer C) will likely have dealt with the original incident(s) that led to the problem being raised. Change management (answer D) will only be involved when a proposed fix needs to be authorized.
34	B	SO 4.4.2 Scope	Proactive problem management involves analysing data, looking for trends and raising problems as a result. Service level management (answer A) may contribute but will not analyse low level incident data. Change management (answer C) does not analyse incident data for trends. Event management (answer D) will look for trends but in event data.

35	A	SO 4.3.2 Scope	'How to' questions and standard changes are good examples of service requests. Answer B is too broad as it covers major changes and projects as well. Answer C has some truth because self-help, web-based tools are often used for service requests, however this is not the only way to submit a request and so is not the BEST description. Answer D describes a change not service request.
36	B	SO 6.3.3 Service desk organizational structure	A local service desk (answer A) serves users in the same location. A virtual service desk (answer C) may be in multiple locations but appears as if it were one desk to the customer. Follow the sun (answer D) is a service desk model where control switches depending on the time of the day. The IT help desk (answer B) is not described in ITIL publications as an organizational structure.
37	B	SO 6.5.1 Operations management role	IT operations control, as part of IT operations management, will provide

			the staff for the operations bridge (this is a front-line monitoring role in a data centre or network operations centre). Request fulfilment (answer C) is a process as so cannot provide staff, Technical and applications management (answers A and D) will work outside of the operation bridge area.
38	C	SD 6.3.2 Generic process owner role	The process owner will define the process strategy (answer A), make sure those who are involved know about it (answer B) and help to identify improvement (answer D). What they are NOT responsible for are IT plans to meet business need.
39	C	SD 3.7.4.1 Designing roles – the RACI model	'I' stands for 'informed' in the RACI matrix, i.e. kept up to date. 'A' in RACI is 'accountable' (answer A). 'R' is 'responsible', which is performing and managing the activity (Answers B and D)
40	A	SS 7.1 Service Automation	Service automation benefits the following areas of service management: Design and modelling Service catalogue Pattern recognition analysis Classification, prioritization and routing Detection, monitoring and optimization The DIKW structure (answer B) relates to knowledge management. Demand management (answer C) would improve pattern recognition and optimization but not detection. Standard changes (answer D) are designed to improve the efficiency and effectiveness of low impact, routine changes.